Some like to play.
Some like to snuggle.

Some grandparents
bake sweet treats

and let you lick the spoon.

Some grandparents grow yummy veggies in the garden

and let you play in the dirt.

Some grandparents take you to the park

and push you high
on the swing.

All grandparents